Drop into the ancient landscape of Britain with this delightful book by Frances Lewis and Adelina Abad-Pedrosa. From ancient hill forts to dramatic cliff tops by the sea, from churches to caves — this book has everything to tempt you and invite you out of your armchair into the spectacular healing landscape of nature and earth energy.

This book provides a beautiful insight into the journey that Frances and Adelina followed as they danced and photographed all the points where the Michael and Mary ley lines meet in Britain. It represents both a personal journey and a journey for the world.

Balancing the male and female energies within ourselves and around the world has the potential to bring us into a saner, more sustainable way of living.

D1209380

THE DIVINE
Dance

In the Sacred Landscape
of Britain

Frances Lewis
&
Adelina Abad-Pedrosa

in the garden Publishing
a media company of
WHAT WOULD LOVE DO INT'L LTD

Copyright © 2012 by Frances Lewis and Adelina Abad-Pedrosa

All rights reserved. No part of this publication may be reproduced in whole or in part, or transmitted in any form by any means electronic, mechanical, magnetic, and photographic including photocopying, recording or by any information storage and retrieval system without prior written permission by the publisher, except for the brief inclusions of quotations in a review.

ISBN: 978-0-9855314-4-7

Library of Congress data available upon request.

Cover and Interior Design by Christine Horner

Published by:

IN THE GARDEN PUBLISHING
P.O. Box 752252
Dayton, OH 45475

www.InTheGardenPublishing.com
www.WhatWouldLoveDoIntl.com

Printed in the United States of America

Table of Contents

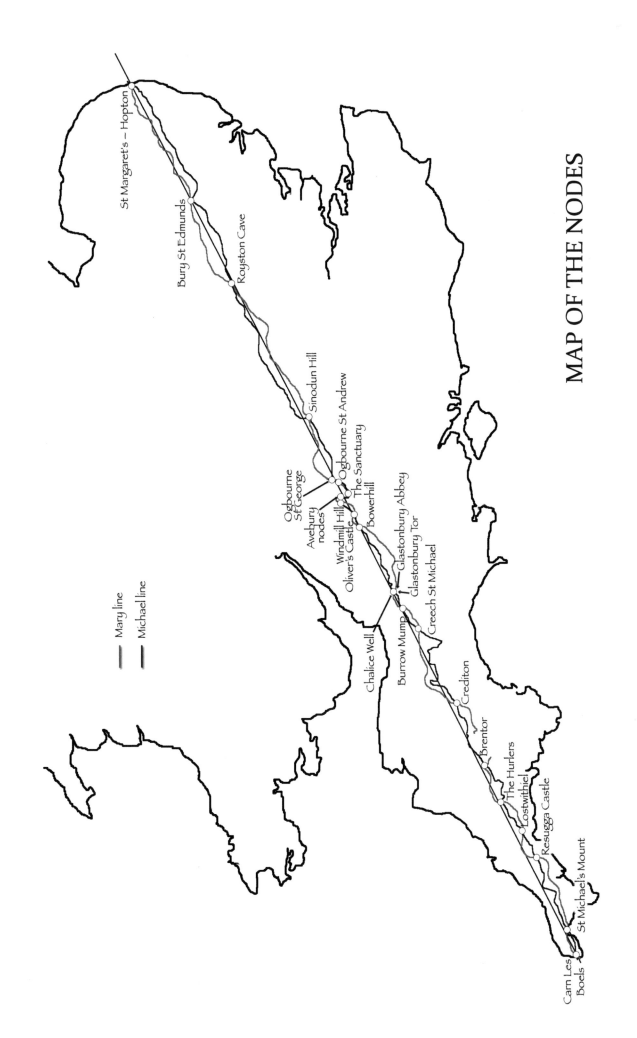

MAP OF THE NODES

Mary line
Michael line

St Margaret's – Hopton
Bury St Edmunds
Royston Cave
Sinodun Hill
Ogbourne St Andrew
Ogbourne St George
The Sanctuary
Avebury nodes
Windmill Hill
Bowerhill
Oliver's Castle
Glastonbury Abbey
Glastonbury Tor
Creech St Michael
Chalice Well
Burrow Mump
Crediton
Brentor
The Hurlers
Lostwithiel
Resugga Castle
St Michael's Mount
Carn Les Boels

FORWARD

When I first saw this very special book I was humbled by the realisation that the dowsing work of two decades ago, which revealed the exquisite subtleties of the dance of the male and female earth energies along the "Michael" Line, has been an inspiration to many talented people to express in their own particular way their understanding of these delicate forces.

Frances and Adelina have combined their superb artistic gifts to produce a beautifully crafted book, which captures the essence of the two weaving energies with all the finely-honed variations of their interactive moods.

These are soft, subtle, but powerful natural energies, which have had a deep and lasting influence on the evolution of our human species.

Minds like those of Frances and Adelina, who recognise the importance of these natural forces and their profound effect on our behaviour, have, through their creative talents, the keys to our cosmic inheritance.

I have a deep understanding and appreciation of the dedication and gritty determination of these two artistic people to produce a book of such quality in these difficult times.

Well done and thank you both so much.

Hamish Miller

Having been approached by Frances and Adelina to be involved in their dancing project at Avebury, I took the risk of dancing for the day. I had occasionally chanted with Frances at a local gathering but did not know her well at all and had not met Adelina before.

I admired the courage and commitment, which both Adelina and Frances were bringing to their journey and was prepared to be the fool and the man to meet them. It is the same risk we each take when we dare to enter into life more fully. It's kind of scary, but it's also a great adventure. And it was fun. When preparing for the dance, Frances and I agreed to fully enter the dance and, through that process, to honour the moment, the spirit of the place and each other.

And it was all simply and profoundly in the dance that day. The dance, when we fully let go into that sacred space is ALL.

JJ Middleway

I have had the honour to witness Frances over many years transform from a shy wallflower who barely had the courage to step onto the dance floor, into the being who dances gloriously across the pages of this book. Colourful, passionate, honest, delicate, and above all a woman stepping forth embracing and offering her dancing journey as a generous gift to her fellow men and women.

Dawn Morgan

Adelina's gift with photography is not only to surprise and delight, but also to include the viewer. She manages to make us feel as if we are there with them participating in the dancing of the Michael and Mary node points and accompanying them on their journey. By capturing the mood of the moment with her careful watchfulness she draws us into their world of balancing the male and female energies in a deeply personal way.

We are immediately captivated by the colour and light in Adelina's arresting photographs, but she also opens up our senses to be receptive towards the less visible such as the air around them. Sometimes cold and damp, other times hot and hazy, we are always made aware of the subtlety of its presence. In her images we are able to hear the sounds, or the silence, and inhale the smells that exude at the moment of the shutter being pressed. She is not just there faithfully recording her subject. She is also adding her own experience. We sense her quietly and intuitively moving around; exploring every angle to intensify the feeling she is receiving, so that we might understand the moment and enjoy it more. She captures the diversity of Frances's connection with her emotions and energies, whether they are playful and joyful or fearful and confused, with an honesty and rawness that can't help but draw us in.

Adelina and Frances have created a unique exploration of the meetings of the Michael and Mary ley lines. With the magical spark of collaborative creativity, they have explored the subtle energies that exist in these special places and interpreted them as visible emotions of both the body and mind. The two have worked as one and it shines through in this joyous celebratory book.

Boo Beaumont

ACKNOWLEDGEMENT

Many thanks to Hamish Miller and Paul Broadhurst for their invaluable guide book *The Sun and the Serpent* that inspired us to make this dancing and photography journey. Also special thanks to Hamish and Ba for welcoming us into their home and for encouraging and supporting us in the creation of this book.

Many thanks to our special guest, JJ Middleway, for engaging with our project so fully in Avebury and for providing his original poem *To Women*, as well as the Arthurian legend *What Do Women Really Want?*

We would also like to express our gratitude to Mahasatvaa Ma Ananda Sarita & Swami Anand Geho for their inspiration with the letter entitled *Tantra: Union of Opposites*. Especially to Sarita for her feedback and her poem *Sacred Waters*, inspired by the Chalice Well section of this book.

Many thanks to Jude Currivan for introducing Frances to the healing power of Avebury and Earth energy.

Great appreciation to Boo Beaumont for the photography tuition, inspiration and guidance that she provided to Adelina, and for her very helpful guidance with the early editing of the photographs in this book.

Many thanks to Dawn Morgan who has been Frances' 5 Rhythms teacher for many years.

We are also very grateful to Andy Beer for his precious and detailed feedback and for his poem *Where the Ocean Meets the Land* (written for this book and inspired by the granite sea cliffs near Lands End, with the waves crashing beneath), which so beautifully embodies the spirit of this book.

Many, many thanks to Christine Horner for seeing the beauty in our book and taking it to a new level of lushness and abundance. We are truly delighted to work with her and to be published by in the garden Publishing.

Last but not least, a special thanks to all those friends who supported us in this project (Penny & Gordon, Penny's brother Richard, Sarah & Steve, Pat) and those people who have help us in a variety of ways along the way.

INTRODUCTION

This book represents both a personal journey and a journey for the world. Balancing the male and female energies within ourselves and around the world has the potential to bring us into a saner, more sustainable way of living. This is what we embraced when we initiated the project of dancing all the points (nodes) where the Michael and Mary lines meet in Britain.

The Michael and Mary lines are ley lines (earth energy lines), which run across southern Britain, from the far west of Cornwall to the east coast of Norfolk. These ley lines link up sacred sites such as St. Michael's Mount, Glastonbury, Avebury and Royston Caves, among many others.

Michael represents the male energy and Mary the female. Together they weave their way through the landscape. Along their way are churches and hills named after Michael and Mary, acknowledging the recognition of these energies in ancient times.

The node points, also called power centres, are the places where ley lines penetrate and leave the earth vertically. They also coincide with the points where the Michael and Mary lines meet and thus, to us, represent the places where the male and female energies are most balanced.

We were inspired by the book *The Sun and the Serpent* by Hamish Miller and Paul Broadhurst. This has been our guide along the way, together with the dowsing rods, allowing us to find the nodes. We gradually developed and learned to trust our dowsing skills as the journey progressed.

There are two natural energies inside each of us, one male and one female. The male energy is characterized by qualities like logic, power, focus, directness, giving, commitment, pushing, excitement and manifestation. The female qualities relate to nurturing, acceptance, softness, meandering, receptivity, creativity, restfulness and peacefulness. If there is an imbalance between them or we don't allow one of them to flow naturally, it becomes very difficult to run our lives in a harmonious and successful way, as we need both to take on the challenges of this life in a loving and purposeful manner. This is key to solving all other imbalances in the world (violence, poverty, conflict, injustice, ecological devastation, etc.).

Our journey was a whole exercise of balancing the male and female energies on many levels; balancing planning and structure with the energy of going with the flow and allowing things to unfold spontaneously. There was often a dance between us – Adelina, the artist, the photographer who wanted the best light (usually that meant getting up at 4:20am and sometimes earlier). Frances, the dancer, who wanted the experience of the dance, was not always so keen on the early morning. Also not keen on dancing more than one node a day (integration time was required as each node had a different message and depth of experience), while Adelina was often holding the more male energy of getting things done with the time available.

Originally we thought it would be great to do the whole adventure in one trip – maybe take 3 months off and dive into the experience. However, we both had demanding work that we enjoyed, so we decided to weave this journey in amongst regular life.

Frances teaches Yoga in Swindon and Adelina was working at the time as a senior analyst for an energy company. What we found was that we required integration time in between nodes, as we were changing, balancing and growing with this journey. Also, our regular life fed into the pilgrimage and vice versa.

So, we had various life adventures alongside this journey of dancing the Michael and Mary node points: relationship ending, 50th birthday, moving house, converting a garage into a yoga studio, demanding work, health problems, exciting work prospects abroad, creating a website and in depth personal development courses are just some of the things we juggled alongside this adventure.

Although the journey was essentially about balancing male and female energies, there were other recurring themes:

• Whose rules do we obey? The church, the landowners, the state or our own?

• Being willing to be seen, to be visible. Maybe be seen as being "weird" and unconventional.

• Honesty and containment. Honesty about what we were doing, if not honest there is no real connection. Protection, containment, we can be honest but do not have to tell everyone everything.

We started this dancing and photography pilgrimage in spring equinox 2006 and completed the journey in autumn equinox 2007. It has been an amazing adventure of inner and outer discovery and we are delighted to offer this book as an insight into what we experienced and discovered. The order in which the nodes are presented here corresponds to the chronological order in which we journeyed through them (not geographical).

This adventure involved lots of walking and an amazing variety of landscapes, from rolling hills to spectacular cliffs with sea views, from churches to caves and an uncovering of an older more ancient landscape of Britain, which we hope you can appreciate in the beauty of the pictures here. We would encourage anyone who is inspired by this book to venture out into this beautiful landscape and look towards the layers of history and mystery right on your doorstep.

WHERE THE OCEAN MEETS THE LAND

There He stands, bold and firm, announcing to the world " I am!"
She laughs at Him, lapping at His feet, teasing and flirting;
He enjoys the attention, holding Himself proud, aloft;
At that, She scorns and mocks Him, as She ebbs away;
Twinges of uncertainty shiver Him, yet He holds steady;
She dances playfully around Him as She floods once more;
He does not begin to understand Her, but still He is present;
Without warning, She becomes a wild, crazed maelstrom;
He shudders at Her wrath and Her power as she lashes Him;
And He knows that one day She will consume Him;
Yet the silence of His being is not shaken;
Rather He declares to Her,
" I am here: from You; with You; in You."
With this She melts around Him and He is gone;
They are no more She and He.

Andy Beer (March, 2010)

THE JOURNEY...

Glastonbury Tor

Southeastern Side of Tor (Somerset)

First dancing trip – the theme was fear.
Fear in the run up to the trip,
fear in the belly and in the back and in the pelvis.

Lots of fear....

Feeling the fear and the memory of fear that many women have.
There is a very real fear of men in the culture and individually.
Fear of male power and aggression out of control.

Gripped with fear.
Dancing on side of Tor at dawn.
Feeling the fear and continuing to move.
Fear of softening into womanliness.
Fear of softening.

*Dancing, moving and being with the feelings of
fear transform it...*

Chalice Well

Gardens at Glastonbury (Somerset)

Wet and wintery, red and lush and dripping.
A robin feeds from the hand of the gatekeeper.

Learning to feel earth energy.
Dancing with a small audience.
Energised from walking and dancing barefoot
in the rain...

SACRED WATERS

The sacred ground gives birth to healing waters,

washing mind and body from impurities born out

of mental divisions.

Male and female energies entwined into christic

consciousness,

blessing the spot as an eternal solace for all

pilgrims of truth.

by Mahasatvaa Ma Ananda Sarita PhD

Glastonbury Abbey

(Somerset)

Who grants permission?
Who sets the rules?

Running, walking, lying in the grass near the High Altar.
Lying face down on the ley line. Deep, deep, relaxation.

Sadness and fear again, fear of intimacy, fear of
surrendering or softening to love.
No real way to connect.
Sadness at the man who wants to commit but has not
been able up until now.
Sadness at the girl who wants to open to love but feels
cheated on and betrayed.
Maybe there is not enough guidance and support.

Sadness at the loss.

Brentor

**Flattened mound near St. Michael's Church
on top of Brentor (Devon)**

∽⊙∾ ℘∾

How to stay centred in the self and connect?
How to keep nourishing ourselves?
Giving up old co-dependency patterns.

Watching footballers devastated and in tears on the pitch.
Male vulnerability,
where is there a place for it?
Sometimes in the arms of their woman.
Competitiveness more easily acceptable for men.
But what of their vulnerability?

SELF NOURISHMENT

If there is light in the soul,

there will be beauty in the person.

If there is beauty in the person,

there will be harmony in the house.

If there is harmony in the house,

there will be order in the nation.

If there is order in the nation,

there will be peace in the world.

(Chinese Proverb)

Crediton

Church of the Holy Cross (Devon)

Waiting, waiting, watching and enjoying the
colourful parade.
Waiting patiently for the bride and the groom to
commit and be on their way...

Commitment? Co-creation?
Creativity, fun, ceremony, celebration.
Are we ready to commit to anything to
completion?
Does it have to be heavy?
Or can it be easy and flowing?
Where is the balance?

All this is part of the journey of creation....

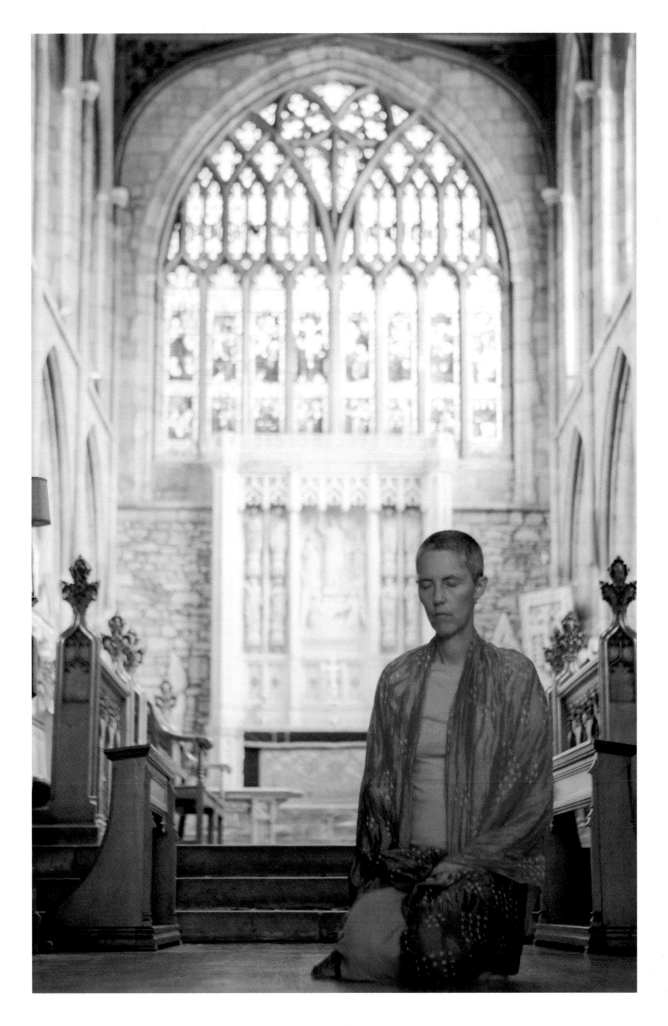

Burrow Mump

Ruined church of St. Michael on the summit of Burrow Mump (Somerset)

All day in some way or another we had been shy of admitting
what we were doing. All day in different ways we have been
secretive or not completely upfront or honest.
This led to us feeling not connected to other people,
feeling stirred-up inside, fearful and anxious.
Fear continued into the dreams that night.

Start a new day and a new way on Sunday.
Walk to the top of the mump.
No longer in the energy of hiding.
Had lovely connections with a family of three generations.
They asked lots of questions about dowsing and energy lines.

Man and his blind son cycled up on a tandem.
Also asked about dowsing and
we encourage them to try the rods.
Lovely, lovely father and son relationship.

Totally different energy today.

Honesty & Connection.

Creech St. Michael

St. Michael's Church (Somerset)

Another wedding just finishing.
Church is after locked...

Slept on the Mary line – delicious deep rest.
Woman brings flowers for her dead husband's grave.
Sat on a bench she provided in his memory.
Another man chats, "Church is not usually locked!"

After a picnic by the river, come back to the church.
Church warden is just locking up again.
He shows us around, the organ, the windows,
the coats of arms...

Hard to connect with the energy of this node.
Too much locking up going on,
locking up and locking out...

Windmill Hill

**Location of neolithic settlement
in Avebury Complex (Wiltshire)**

Easy to find.
Clouds clear as the sun comes up.
Amazing dance and chant, dressed in gold.

Singing "Whatever you can do or dream about,
just begin it. Boldness has genius, power and
magic in it."

Personal reluctance to turn up at every level.
It might rain – let's stay at home.
It is cloudy – don't take the gold trousers.
My feet are cold. Let's go home.

*Who is for continuing and staying with it
until completion...?*

Sinodun Hill

Fenced off hill fort (Oxfordshire)

Masses and masses of dripping fruit where the Mary line
flowed.
Yellow plums, blackberries, small red plums and
elderberries everywhere.
Sunny, warm, smell of ripe delicious fruit.
We began to acclimatise to this place of warmth and
abundance.

Risk tree branches falling on us.
This was a very beautiful and special place.
Shame that we had not been able to fully enjoy being
there without worrying about falling branches and being
seen...

Ogbourne St. George

Mound in a field (Wiltshire)

This was a little bit difficult for us to find.
But when we found it, it was undeniable.
Steep mound inside a field.
Surrounded by a barbed wire fence.
With small bushy trees growing on it.
Thorny trees.
Very well protected...

Climbed over and through the barbed wire fences.
Climbed up through low growing thorny trees to
the top of the mound.
A blue rope to help climbers up and down.
Sat perched on the top, caution prickly branches...

Delightful spot

with views

and very

special energy.

Very welcome picnic.

Carn Les Boel

Rock formation near Lands End (Cornwall)

Mist, mist everywhere – not sure if we were really there.
Dressed in orange and danced in the mist.
A dance of fear.
Fear of being seen.
Fear of being powerful.
Fear of speaking up and being heard.
No, no, no, it was not the dance of fear.
Fear was there, but it was the dance of breaking free.
It was a powerful dance.

The sound of the sea crashing on the rocks below and
still we could not see through the early morning mist.
Deep, deep mist and deep, deep sea.
As we sat, rested and digested, the mist very gradually
lifted to reveal the most spectacular scenery.
Dramatic cliffs and clear jade blue sea.

.

A seal playing in the water by the rocks.
Magnificent and spectacular beyond words.
Walk down to the cove for a swim in the clear cold sea.
What an amazing way to start the day!

Royston Cave

Bell shaped chamber, 30 feet high, cut in solid chalk (Hertfordshire)

Spectacular, spectacular chalk cave under the
street of this small town.
Carvings of both Pagan and Christian symbols.

Warm and damp.
Took a risk and asked for permission.
Took off my shoes and got into the dance.
Time limited – now-or-never feeling...

Magic and mystery.

Bury St. Edmunds

Abbey ruins and gardens (Suffolk)

∽◎∾

Today, of all days, there was a celebration of 400
years of connection with America. Main focus was
on celebrating the military connection of both
countries...
So many people around, this was not going to be a
private dance...
Dance in the Abbey ruins in the area of the choir.
Occasionally people passed by.
Gradually becoming more bold about continuing with
the dance.

*Still feeling some lack of confidence in being bold,
but being bold nevertheless...*

St. Margaret's Hopton

**Church ruin, covered in ivy and
surrounded by a tall wire fence (Norfolk)**

Health and safety keeping us out.

Danced in the drizzle with the outside of the fence.
Very, very disappointed at not being able to get in.
Very self conscious of dancing in a housing estate.
Rain getting heavier.

Discussion about power. Who has the power?
How do we give away our power?

The dance might stimulate fear in others.
That is their fear, not ours.
But aware our fears could become mingled.

Once again themes of power, fear, being visible...

Ogbourne St. Andrew

**Mound in church yard surrounded
by tall trees (Wiltshire)**

Dark and cool with speckles of light coming
through the trees.
Touching the leaves, the trees, the earth and
the fir cones.

Tears were cried for the delicateness of the
earth and the delicateness of me.
Crying gentle tears, connecting deeply with
my vulnerability and my delicateness.
Slowing down and connecting with the leaves,
the trees, the earth and the stones.
Connecting with the air and the sparkly
sunlight of the summer eve.

Delicate, delicate, sensitive fingertips.
Delicate, delicate womb.
Delicate, delicate, delicate earth.
Delicate, delicately tenderness flows.

Tears dripping gently down the neck.
Oh, how we have to soften and slow down to connect
with our souls!
Slow and delicate is the dance of this mound.
Slow and delicate with love and tears.

Bowerhill

Ancient spring in housing estate (Wiltshire)

The sunlight was beginning to fade.
We struggled through the brambles.
This node is in an area of neglect.
It has a feel of neglect.

The dance here was of trying to find the light.
The light coming through the trees was limited.
Sounds of children playing nearby, but we felt
hidden in another layer of life.

Some node points are so healthy and vibrant in earth
energy that we receive intensely from just being there.
This ancient spring was neglected and not appreciated.
There was decay and damp and prickles that scratched us.
This node felt in need of something from us.
A beautiful altar to earth, air, fire and water.

Rest, rest, restful spring.
We can not always dance high energy on the top of a hill.
We require times of rest and what might seem like neglect.
Yes, even neglect is okay in the scheme of things.
It means we are not over-busy with our tidying up and
rearranging,
coming and going.

Try sitting on a pile of neglect for a while.
It is okay to not always be tidy...

Oliver's Castle

Ancient hill fort (Wiltshire)

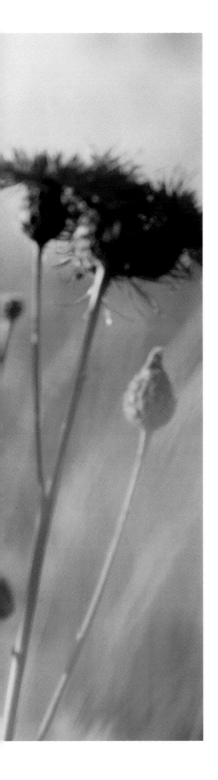

A stunning, pink sun was quickly arising.
We rushed to the node, quick, quick into the dance.

Dancing angry, dancing cross.
This time the tears and the sounds were loud.
Shouting, crying, screaming, groaning into the wind.

No more to the ways I neglect
and abuse myself still.
No, no, no!!!

On the top of this hill at dawn with the cold wind blowing
and the bright sun rising
and the most expansive view.

The Sanctuary

**Prehistoric site on Overton Hill,
Avebury Complex (Wiltshire)**

Here is the dance of exhaustion.
Tired – slow – heavy – exhausted movements.
Don't rush, don't push the energy.
If there is no energy then rest.
Rest in the dance.
Stretch and move and yawn and rest and roll and
surrender to the soft ground.
Soft, soft and slightly damp soft grass.
Cool morning air, expansive cloudy sky.
Don't push, don't pretend.
Just rest and roll and surrender to the soft damp
earth and the great expansive sky.
Soft sweet sounds of OM blending with the sky.

St. Michael's Mount

**Legendary tidal island with castle
on the top (Cornwall)**

The node is in the most spectacular spot.
There are four ley lines all crossing at the same point.
Michael and Mary and Apollo and Athena.
Very powerful and beautiful place.

Soft, green, lush grass to dance on with magnificent
rocks all around.
Clear, clear blue sea and sky.
The dance was easy and tired, also a dance of
boundaries, held in a circle of rocks.
Some anxiety about being seen again - it is okay to
break the rules?

Resugga Castle

Iron age hill fort (Cornwall)

❧

Early, early morning dance.
The field had been cut for hay, we think.
Unbelievable softness to walk in.
Deep, deep, softness underfoot.
Damp, damp, dew everywhere.
Dancing and chanting at dawn.
Reluctantly rising before the dawn.
Then joyfully playing and participating in the
wonderful sunrise.

Lostwithiel

St. Bartholomew's Church in Lostwithiel (Cornwall)

Deciding to attend the Sunday morning service.
Incredibly welcomed by the priest and many of the churchgoers.
Creative priest.
Left feeling the emphasis was on all of us as sinners.

Hurlers

**Three stone circles on top of moor
(Cornwall)**

High ground, open moorland.
Middle of middle circle is node point.
Evening dance.
People around.
Quite a public dance.
Not so much angst about being seen,
although not completely free while being
watched.

Male and female symbolising stones in the centre of the middle stone circle at The Hurlers.

The Avebury Henge

Avebury Complex (Wiltshire)

Avebury is one of the most important sites because here the male and the female lines run together from the Cove through the Obelisk to The Devil's Chair, incorporating two node points (usually Michael and Mary lines weave in and out of each other, but they do not normally run together, except here).

We decided a man and a woman were required to dance this part of the journey.

Our special guest, JJ Middleway, engaged fully with our project in Avebury and also provided his own poem *To Woman* and a very relevant story *What Do Women Really Want?*, as presented in the following pages.

AVEBURY IS IN MY HEART

Whatever time of day or season of the year, this magical and mysterious place that has been held sacred for many thousands of years inspires and nurtures me on every level of my being - as it has done over millennia and continues to do for untold numbers of others, too.

The great henge and stone circle of Avebury is a perfect centre-point to celebrate the yearly cycle and the great cosmic dance of the Sun, Moon and Earth. My beloved husband, Tony, and myself try to visit Avebury at the dawn of these days as, no doubt, our ancestors did. We are often - and especially in the winter months! - the only two humans there, along with the ageless stones, the standing people we call trees, the communities of crows that inhabit them and the discarnate guardians whose ancient and wise voices may be heard in the quiet time, as night gives way to day.

One morning however, as we walked silently towards the cove, we saw a woman and a man - Frances & JJ. We watched as they wove a gentle trance of compassion and care around each other, blessed by the benediction of Avebury's magic.

They melded with each other and the land as the Sun rose in all his glory to herald another day. And we, as witnesses, also felt our souls rise in love and joy and gratitude in the universal heart that enfolds us all.

Afterwards, we left as silently as we had come...

by Jude Currivan, PhD

Avebury - The Cove

Avebury - The Obelisk

Dance the message of ease – not wild orgasms
as could be expected – but the dance of ease.

Easy intimacy.
Easy honesty.
Easy play and sensuality.

Ease, Ease, Ease!

WHAT DO WOMEN REALLY WANT?

Young King Arthur was ambushed and imprisoned by the monarch of a neighbouring kingdom. The monarch could have killed him, but was moved by Arthur's youthful happiness. So the monarch offered him freedom, as long as he could answer a very difficult question.

Arthur would have one month to figure out the answer. If, after a month, he still had no answer, he would be killed.

The question Arthur was asked, " What do women really want?"

Such a question would perplex even the most knowledgeable man, and to young Arthur, it seemed an impossible query. Well, since it was better than death, he accepted the monarch's proposition to have an answer by month's end.

He returned to his kingdom and began to poll everybody; the princess, the priests, the wise men, the court jester. But, no one could give him a satisfactory answer. What most people did tell him was to consult the old witch, as only she would know the answer. The price would be high, since the witch was famous throughout the kingdom for the exorbitant prices she charged.

The last day of the month arrived and Arthur had no alternative but to talk to the witch. She agreed to answer his question, but he would have to accept her price first. The old witch wanted to marry Gawain, the most noble of the Knights of the Round Table and Arthur's closest friend. Young Arthur was horrified! The witch was hunchbacked and awfully hideous, had only one tooth and smelled disgusting. He had never run across such a repugnant creature.

Arthur refused to force his friend to marry her and have to endure such a burden. Gawain, upon learning of the proposal, spoke with Arthur. He told him that nothing was too big of a sacrifice compared to Arthur's life and the preservation of the Round Table. Hence, their wedding was proclaimed, and the witch was honour-bound to answer Arthur's question:

The answer: What a woman really wants is to be respected and to be in charge of her own life.

Everyone instantly knew that the witch had uttered a great truth and that Arthur's life would be spared. And so it was. The neighbouring monarch spared Arthur's life and granted his freedom.

What a wedding Gawain and the witch had! Arthur was torn between relief and anguish.

Gawain was proper as always, gentle and courteous. The old witch put her worst manners on display and made everyone uncomfortable.

Eventually the wedding night approached. Gawain, steeling himself for a horrific night, entered the bedroom. But what a sight awaited!

The most beautiful woman he'd ever seen lay before him! Gawain was astounded and asked what had happened. The beauty replied that since he had been so kind to her, half the time she would be her horrible, deformed self, and the other half, she would be her beautiful maiden self. Which would he want her to be during the day and which during the night? What a cruel question?

Gawain began to think of his predicament. During the day a beautiful woman to show off to his friends, but at night, in the privacy of his home, an old spooky witch? Or would he prefer having by day a hideous witch, but by night a beautiful woman to enjoy many intimate moments?

What would you do?

Noble Gawain replied that he would let her choose for herself. Upon hearing this, she announced that she would be beautiful all time, because he had respected her and had let her be in charge of her own life.

Arthurian Legend

TO WOMAN

Inspired by the Goddess in one woman and
dedicated to the Goddess in all women

(* circa 1993)

Oh, Lady thou art fair of face.

Blessed with beauty, poised with Grace.

Soft sun light permeates your form,

As you reflect the golden dawn.

Contrasting with the silvery sheen

of gilded moonlight in between.

Stunning is the luminescence

of your elusive lunar essence.

Let me enfold you in a cloak

of sumptuous threaded leaves of oak.

Spun of the sun's own gossamer

Thus is crafted love's amour.

Oh, lady let me hear you sing

As I in heaven strum the string.

The one stringed harp of joyous bliss

The magic all pervasive kiss.

To feel your touch

To touch your feel.

To breathe your breath

my heart it reels.

Then sink and swim

And swim and sink.

We teeter on the very brink

of life's ecstatic wondrous chord.

Before we plunge into the ford

And submerge souls in radiant throng

we've found the place where we belong,

me in you and you in me ~

Transcending all duality.

In honour of the Sacred dance we were at
Avebury for Autumn Equinox, 2007.

Yours in love and blessings on behalf of
the sacred male.

JJ Middleway

Avebury - Devil's Chair

Node just before the lines leave the Avebury
Henge between two big stones.
One of them is known as the Devil's Chair.
It's a place for invoking fertility.

This felt like a dance of honouring both the male and the female, the masculine and the feminine.
Frances asked JJ the question:
"What do men want by way of honouring?"
Nourished and seen by the man, she became incredibly generous as a woman towards this man.

ADELINA ABAD-PEDROSA

Adelina Abad-Pedrosa was born in Spain. A PhD in Chemical and Environmental Engineering brought her work in the sectors of consulting, engineering and energy markets.

Currently, she explores her true nature, following the call of each moment, geographically and in all other aspects of life.

As a photographer, Adelina aims to capture all facets of life and the human experience in her images. Her work is often defined as having the healing power of conscious witnessing. She also ventures into the fields of documentary, portraiture, travel, artistic, nature and corporate photography. In 2005, her photography won the portrait award by ICIA (Bath University). Her work has been exhibited in magazines, solo and group exhibitions.

For more information, please visit www.adelinaabad.com

FRANCES LEWIS

Frances Lewis is a courageous dancer of truth and wisdom. She is regularly willing to drop again into a softer more vulnerable way of being with herself and with others in the world.

She is a truly inspirational woman with a passion for expressive dance, deep peace, nature and ecology.

Frances teaches Yoga and loves to create sacred space in which to experience Yoga, be it in the middle of a town or in deep nature. Space clearing has been a major part of her journey of transformation along with yoga and dance.

More recently she has been offering womb healing visualisation as part of a growing movement to honour the feminine more fully.

For more information, please visit www.franceslewis.co.uk

OTHER PROJECTS

Frances and Adelina have also created a pack of beautiful and bold Chakra Cards that have inspired others to introduce changes in their life.

The powerful simplicity of the pictures and the words and symbols, summing up the essence of each chakra, make these cards a unique practical tool. www.franceslewis.co.uk/shop/

REFERENCES & LINKS

The Sun and the Serpent by Hamish Miller and Paul Broadhurst (ISBN 0951518313).

Hamish Miller was a dowser, metal sculptor and author. He read engineering at Edinburgh and through his books, talks and workshops, his work on earth energies has earned him an international reputation. www.hamishmiller.co.uk

Paul Broadhurst is an author, photographer and researcher into mythology and sacred landscapes. www.mythospress.co.uk

JJ Middleway is a druid and a master of ceremonies. www.druidry.org/druid-way/resources/celebrants

Mahasatvaa Ma Ananda Sarita PhD is a world renowned Tantra teacher and author. She lived 26 years in India learning Tantra, Meditation and Holistic Healing, and has been teaching all over the world since 1990. Her work is based in the UK, and the branches of her Tantra tree have spread far and wide through a highly qualified and dedicated team of teachers. www.tantra-essence.com

Dr. Jude Currivan PhD is a cosmologist, planetary healer, international award-winning Hay House author, visionary and educator. www.judecurrivan.com

Boo Beaumont is an award winning X Ray Artist, Filmmaker and Portrait Photographer with her work in many major collections including the National Portrait Gallery in London. www.boobeaumont.org

Dawn Morgan has worked with dance and movement since 1991. She is trained to teach both levels of Gabrielle Roth's 5 Rhythms. Her M.A. in Dance and Somatic Education, has encouraged her to weave the practice of different movement disciplines into a unique offering. She teaches classes in the UK and abroad. www.shapeshift.co.uk

The 5 Rhythms are a beautiful dancing map of the movement of energy. The structure guides you through different ways of moving and offers you the freedom to discover and deepen your own dance. It is an invitation and an initiation into ecstatic free dance. You are playfully invited to physicalise your energy; emotional, physical, spiritual, whatever arises in the moment of moving. This active meditation practice brings about a natural vitality and an awakening to the movement and interconnectedness of all life.

Andy Beer is a mystic, a reiki master and an eternal nomad, wandering aimlessly, playing with energy, meditation and life. He offers satsangs, retreats, reiki training, writes books and whatever else comes to him along the way. www.abeing.org